SPORTS CARS

OFF TO THE RACES

PETER & NILDA SESSLER

The Rourke Press, Inc.
Vero Beach, Florida 32964

We recognize that some words, model names and designations
mentioned herein, are the property of the trademark holder. We use them
for identification purposes only. This is not an official publication.

PHOTO CREDITS
© Daimler Chrysler Corporation: pages 19, 22;
© Firestone Tire Company: page 21; © Peter Sessler: cover, pages 4, 6, 7,
9, 10, 13; © PSR (Rich Dole): pages 12, 15, 16, 18

EDITORIAL SERVICES:
Susan Albury

Library of Congress Cataloging-in-Publication Data

Sessler, Peter C., 1950-
    Sports cars / Peter Sessler, Nilda Sessler.
        p. cm. — (Off to the races)
    Includes index.
    Summary: Discusses sport car racing and how it differs from other kinds
of auto racing and describes various sport cars.
    ISBN 1-57103-282-7
    1. Sport cars Juvenile literature. 2. Automobile racing Juvenile literature.
[1. Sport cars. 2. Automobiles, Racing.] I. Sessler, Nilda, 1951- . II. Title. III.
Series: Sessler, Peter C., 1950- Off to the races.
GV1029.S423 1999
796.72—dc21
                                                                99-13826
                                                                     CIP

Printed in the USA

◼︎◻︎◼︎ TABLE OF CONTENTS
◻︎◼︎◻︎

▞ WHAT IS SPORTS CAR RACING?

Sports car racing was always very popular in Europe but it did not catch on in the United States until the early 1960s. Before that time, sports car racing was done mostly by people who raced for fun.

Originally, sports cars were small two-seat cars that came from England. Today, the name *sports car* is used to describe many different types of cars.

 Can-Am cars can go from 0-60 mph in 2.75 seconds and 0-140 mph in 10.2 seconds.

Porsche cars have been raced since the 1950s and they have a long winning record. This 1986 Porsche now races in vintage car races, where only older race cars are allowed to race.

In 1963, the first professional sports car race series, the United States Road Racing Championship (USRRC), had its first race at Daytona, Florida. In 1966, two more race series came into being, the Trans-Am (Trans-American) and Can-Am (Canadian-American) Series.

Professional road racing became popular in the late 1960s with cars such as this Can-Am Series Lola T-70.

One of the best American sports car racers was the Ford GT-40, which won the famous Le Mans 24-hour race from 1966 to 1969.

In the Trans-Am Series, cars like Mustangs and Camaros were raced. In the Can-Am Series, all-out race cars were raced. Sports car racing was slowly becoming popular.

♦ SPORTS CAR SANCTIONING BODIES

The Sports Car Club of America (SCCA) was formed in 1944 and today it holds over 2,000 races every year. Professional Sports Car Racing (PSR) was formed in 1976 and holds hundreds of races each year.

The SCCA and PSR are called **sanctioning** (SANK shun ing) bodies and are responsible for making the rules the cars race under. They make sure the cars are safe, and they also try to make the cars in each class as equal as possible. In this way, the driver's skill makes it possible for him to win, instead of having a faster car.

SCCA and PSR set the rules by which cars can race. In PSR's Speedvision Series, the cars are almost exactly the same as the ones you can buy from your local dealer, such as the Mustang Cobra "R" model.

OPEN-WHEEL CARS

Sports car racing also includes open-wheel cars. These cars don't have fenders and look like small Indy cars. Unlike Indy cars that race mostly on oval tracks, these cars also race on road circuits.

Open-wheel racing is a great training ground for drivers to get experience before they go on to race the ultra-fast Indy-type cars.

World Sport Car Series cars have engines that produce over 675 horsepower.

Open-wheel race cars are raced in both SCCA and PSR. They race mostly on road circuits and are a good training ground for future Indy car drivers.

▟▛ COVERED-WHEEL CARS

The biggest and fastest cars are from the SCCA's Can-Am Series and PSR's World Sports Car Series. These are two-seat open cockpit cars that use custom-made bodies and frames. They are really sleek looking!

This Momo Ferrari is raced in PSR's World Sport Car Series.

Corvettes have been raced since the day they were first made. This 1998 Corvette races in SCCA's Trans-Am Series.

The GT cars are slightly slower. These look like the ones you can buy at the local car dealer and include the Dodge Viper, Chevrolet Corvette, Acura NSX, and many others.

PSR also has a series for grand sports cars such as the Mustang Cobra R, Porsche 968, Toyota Supra, Camaro SS, and Firebird Formula. Except for using special tires and having safety equipment installed, these cars are the same as those you can buy at the dealership.

 From 1966 to 1998, Chevrolet-engined cars have won 134 Can-Am races, Porsche has won 16, and Ford has won 5.

Sports cars are raced on tracks that have hills, turns, bumps, and lots of straightaways.

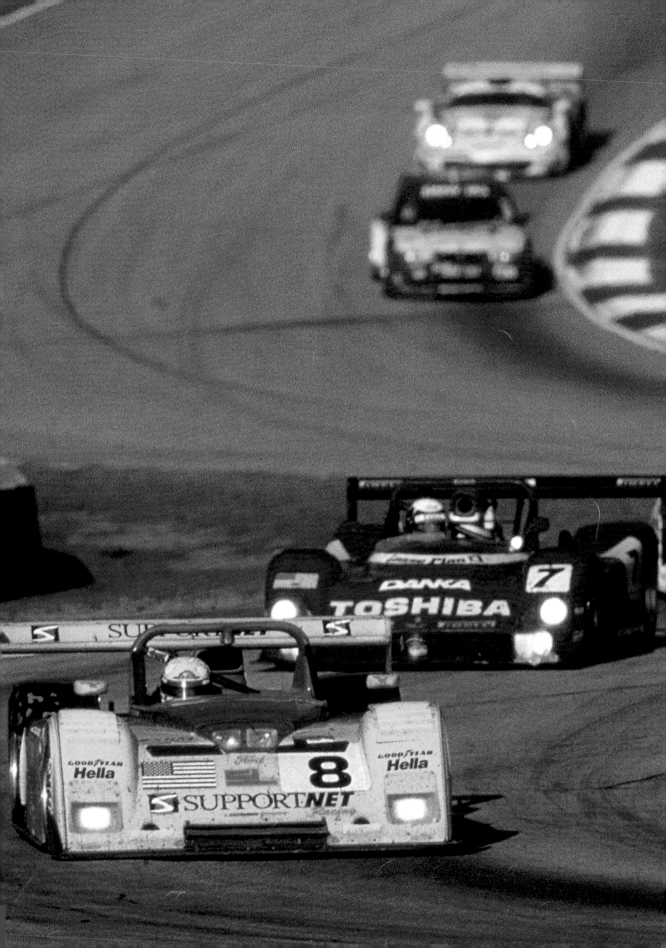

■■ THE TRACKS

There are some big differences between sports car racing and other kinds of racing, such as stock or Indy cars.

Sports cars race mostly on road circuits. These tracks resemble country roads with lots of curves, hills, and straights. Some tracks are only 1-1/2 miles long. Others are longer. The longest road circuit tracks are over 8 miles long.

Some sports cars race at night so they have headlights that work. They also race in all kinds of weather.

Besides road circuits, sports cars also race on **"street circuits"** (STREET SIR cuts). Streets are blocked off in certain cities to make a temporary racetrack. Los Angeles and Detroit have races there every year.

Sports cars also race at night and because most tracks aren't lit, the cars must have headlights.

⬛⬜ IT'S RACE TIME!

Drivers usually arrive with their cars at the track early in the week. This gives the mechanics time to make **adjustments** (ad JUST mentz) to the car so that it will run perfectly during the race. It also gives the driver enough time to practice and to get to know the track.

Here the WSC cars are lined up, ready to take the green flag. The slower GT cars are in the back.

On long races, the cars have to come into the pits to get gas and have their tires changed. Here drivers also switch, because this is a 24-hour race.

Next comes **qualifying** (KWA la fi ing). Each car goes on the track for warm-up laps and then runs several laps to see how fast it can go around the track. The fastest cars get to start at the front. The "pole" position, which is the inside left of the front row, is given to the fastest car.

A **pace car** (PACE kar) leads the race cars around the track for a few warm-up laps. As soon as the race officials see that everything is fine, the starter waves the green flag and the race is on!

Some sports car races are very long and can last 24 hours. In these races, the cars are driven by two and sometimes three drivers, each taking turns. On these and other long races, the cars have to come into the pits many times to get more gas, to change tires, or to make repairs.

Finally, the checkered flag is waved and the race is over. The winning driver takes the car to the victory lane to get his trophy and prize money.

After the race is over, the race teams load the cars back onto their trucks and travel on to the next racetrack. At the end of the year, the driver who has won the most races becomes champion.

It takes a lot of driving skill to pass other cars on this twisty and crowded track.

▚ **GLOSSARY**

adjustments (ad JUST mentz) — minor or small changes

pace car (PACE kar) — an automobile that leads the field of race cars through a pace lap but does not participate in the race

qualifying (KWA la fi ing) — a way to get the best starting position

sanctioning (SANK shun ing) — the rules of racing

street circuits (STREET SIR cuts) — a temporary racecourse made by blocking streets so that regular traffic is not allowed on the roads

CONVERSION TABLE

60 miles per hour........97 kilometers per hour	1-1/2 miles ....2415 meters
140 miles per hour....225 kilometers per hour	8 miles ....13 kilometers

After racing for 24 hours, you can be sure the drivers of the 1998 Le Mans winning Dodge Viper are pretty tired—but they are happy, too!

◼️ INDEX

FURTHER READING

Find out more about racing with these helpful books and organizations:

- *Motorsports America.* 1998
- Ulrich Upietz, *World Sportscar Racing '94.* 1994
  This book covers sports car racing in USA, Europe and Japan in 1994.

- PSR's Official Site: www.professionalsportscar.com
- SCCA's Official Site: www.scca.org